Essex, New York
Architecture

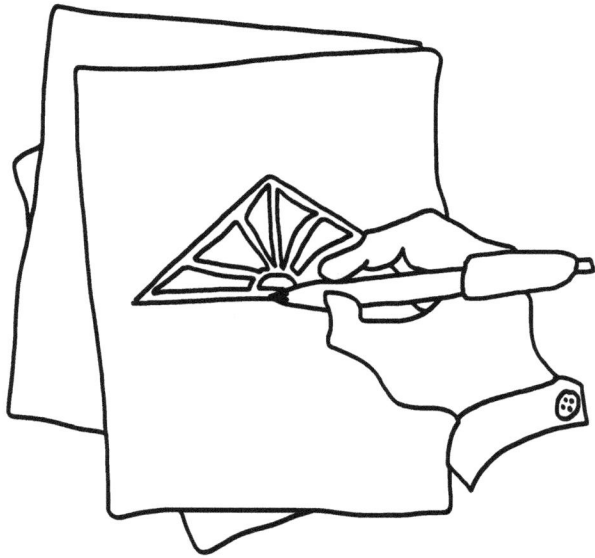

Essex, New York
Architecture
A Doodler's Field Guide

Powered by Essex on Lake Champlain
Edited by G^{eo} Davis & Katie Shepard
Doodled by G^{eo} Davis

To receive an email newsletter about Essex on Lake Champlain subscribe at www.essexonlakechamplain.com/subscribe

Published in the United States by Essex Editions.

ISBN-13: 978-0-9967870-0-0
ISBN-10: 0-996787-00-3

Essex Editions
Post Office Box 25
Essex, New York 12936
www.essexeditions.com
contact@essexeditions.com

In memory of Sid Couchey
whose Essex illustrations will
forever inspire and entertain.

Contents

Appendix

Afterword

Introduction

There's a wonderland of beauty,
One that has ten thousand charms,
At Essex, old Essex-on-Champlain;
Its attractions grip and hold you
Like some giant lover's arms,
Dear Essex, dear Essex-on-Champlain.
~ George Orlia Webster, "Essex-on-Champlain"

Reverend Webster captured the blissful siren call of Essex, New York in a 1929 hymn that still rings true nearly a century later. The hamlet grows more handsome and more beguiling with each passing season, and yet this pastoral enclave nestled between Lake Champlain and the Adirondacks was not always so tranquil.

In the early 19th century Essex was a bustling maritime port. Local merchants prospered, and the population increased, fueling a brief building boom.

Handsome residential and commercial buildings married popular architectural styles with local construction materials.

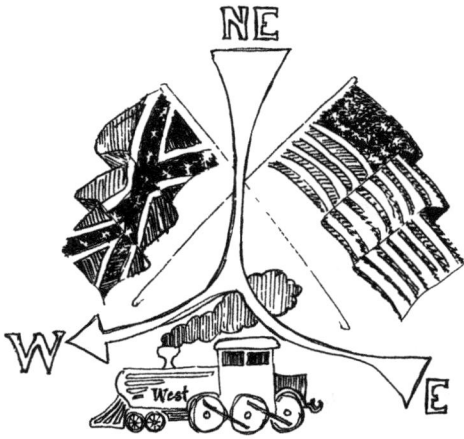

But the business and building boom was short lived. The Civil War, shifting migration trends, and the arrival of railroad transportation stalled growth. New construction diminished, and existing buildings were reused and repurposed. Declining commerce and population fortunately (if unintentionally) preserved many historic buildings in Essex.

"[Essex] is neither a museum or a restoration. It has been preserved intact by the events of its history..." ~ George F. McNulty and Margaret Scheinin, Essex: The Architectural Heritage

In the early 20th century Essex became popular as a tourist destination for seasonal visitors drawn by the leisurely pace and abundant natural resources. In 1975 the hamlet was added to the United States National Register of Historic Places in recognition of its well preserved architecture.

"Essex is especially known for its picturesque Greek Revival architecture enhanced by its location along a scenic lakeshore set among rolling farmlands all within sight of the Adirondack Mountains. This combination of architectural integrity and *environmental purity makes it one of the most intact early-19th-century villages in America still existing today." ~ David C. Hislop Jr., Images of America: Essex on Lake Champlain*

Many of the most architecturally significant buildings within the hamlet of Essex are included on the following pages. We hope that our brief introductions and whimsical illustrations will inspire your curiosity and creativity. We hope that you will fill the white spaces in this book with your own doodles. Enjoy!

You are invited to
Explore and doodle
Essex, New York
Architecture.
To accept, doodle
Your name below.

You might want to include your address
or telephone # in case you misplace
your book. That way a nice person can
return it (with a few extra doodles!)

Warning

This book will [probably] not turn you into an architect...

In fact, if you're already an architect, consider gifting this book to somebody who isn't. Somebody filled with more architectural wonder than wisdom. Somebody with more architectural questions than answers. Somebody curious and lighthearted enough to:

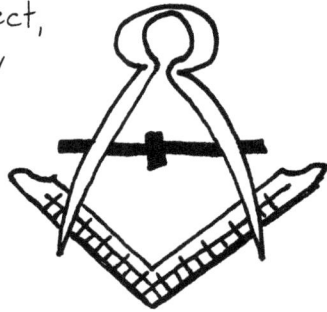

- explore Essex architecture without assumptions;
- doodle Essex architecture without inhibitions;
- and discover Essex architecture in a whole new way.

Whether this is your first or your hundred and first encounter with Essex architecture, immersing and experimenting is not for reiterating what you already know. It's for exploring and discovering what you don't know.

"By Engaging our senses and responding to the tactile and sensuous qualities of the city or town in which we live we lose our feeling of separateness and enter into direct participation with our world, both physically and emotionally." ~ Keri Smith, The Guerilla Art Kit

"We need to move, to feel like we're making something with our bodies, not just our heads... That's what's so great about creative work: If we just start going through the motions... the motion kickstarts our brain into thinking." ~ Austin Kleon, Steal Like an Artist

Why Doodle?

"The once flourishing spirit of commercial enterprise left in its wake a visible heritage that can be read in the buildings and streets of Essex." ~ Essex Community Heritage Organization, "Essex: An architectural guide."

Doodling is a playful way to "read" the intriguing architectural narrative in Essex. Certainly there are more learned resources to consult as your interest in the architectural heritage evolves (see suggestions for further reading at the end of this book), but curiosity is not always piqued by formal discourse or scholastic inquiry.

Sometimes a doodle can teach you more than a dissertation. Or at least it can awaken your wonder and imagination.

Doodling your way along Essex's tree-lined streets and waterfront will envelope you in "a wonderland of beauty... like some giant lover's arms."

"We shall not cease from exploration
And the end of all our exploring
Will be to arrive where we started
And know the place for the first time."
~ T.S. Eliot, Four Quartets

What will you discover (or rediscover) by doodling this collection of old buildings? How will your perspective shift? How will your appreciation and understanding deepen?

And most important of all, will you take creative risks with your doodles? Will you laugh at yourself when your doodles are goofy? Will you celebrate when your doodles are jolly?

As you immerse yourself in the visual stories lurking behind clapboard and brick and stone, we hope that this book will prove useful as a field guide to help you doodle your adventure. Or at least as inspiration to immerse yourself in Essex architecture in a capricious new way. Enjoy!

Doodle Tools & Techniques

It's time to doodle your way around Essex. See the map at the end of this book to help guide you! (Buildings are numbered in the order that they appear in this book.) Put on your walking shoes and grab your favorite doodle tools.

Or better yet, experiment with new ways of doodling. If your go-to doodling device is normally a pad and pencil, it might be time to switch things up. And I don't mean fancy charcoals or state-of-the-art digital tablets either.

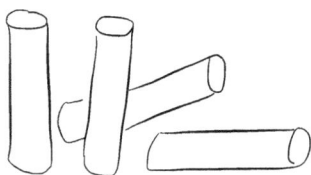

You don't need expensive art supplies to become a doodler. Far from it! There's almost always something handy to doodle. Here are just a few ideas to get you started:

- a stack of scrap paper or a pad
- pencil, marker, crayons or chalk
- napkins or recycled envelopes
- finger paints
- tracing paper

It's fun to experiment with unfamiliar doodle tools, but

sometimes you need to mix it up even more. Sometimes you need to jumpstart your imagination with a whole new approach to image making. Forget pencil and paper for a moment and consider all of the creative ways to doodle with food and other "non-art supplies".

What about a toothpick and ground pepper doodle? Or a chopstick dipped in soy sauce? Here are some possibilities to try when the "adults" aren't watching:

- a freshly used tea bag makes great "ink" on a napkin
- so do coffee, cranberry juice (even wine) on paper place mats
- ketchup (or bright yellow mustard) on your plate
- a noodle doodle would be challenging but oh-so cool

And that's just food!

CAUTION: Some of the doodling techniques listed above *might* qualify as "playing with your food". Also, you may want to snap a picture when you're done rather than framing the original.

ketchup

Here are some ideas that are less likely to get you banished to the children's table:

- finger or stick in wet sand at the beach
- arranging pebbles, twigs or acorns

- wet finger on dry surface (before it dries)
- food coloring on snow (best to avoid yellow)
- fingertip on dirty car windows (or foggy mirrors)
- digital doodles on your phone or tablet

The possibilities are endless!

"Creativity is not a talent. It is a way of operating."
~ John Cleese

How To Use This Book

1. Doodle. Fill the white spaces in this book with your creativity!

2. Be curious. Don't just look. Wonder. Question. Hypothesize. Explore. Shift your perspective. Look around Essex as if it's your first visit. Look closer. Or step further away. Find a high perch, or sit on the ground. Pretend you're somebody else, and doodle in their "style."

3. Unlearn. Don't let your knowledge limit you. Doodle what you don't know. Doodle what intrigues you. Doodle what perplexes you. Doodle the unknowable.

4. Experiment. Doodle contours. Doodle details. Doodle patterns and textures and repetition and symmetry and the patina of time.

5. Take risks. Doodle in public. Doodle in the dark. Doodle with unusual materials. Vary you doodle technique. (See the Doodle Tools & Techniques section for ideas.)

6. Have fun. Laugh at your doodles. Invite others to laugh with you. And encourage them to create doodles of their own so you can laugh at each other.

13

7. Relax. Don't get aggravated. Start over if you want, but don't give up. Remember, there are no mistakes, only quirky doodles.

8. Surprise yourself. Before long you just might create a doodle that you really love. Don't expect it, but celebrate these creative gifts when they happen.

9. Skip around. The order of this book is not important. Start wherever you want, and feel free to ignore doodle suggestions or even make up your own.

10. Share your doodles with the world. Use the hashtag #EssexNY on Facebook, Pinterest, Instagram, Twitter, etc. And remember to show us what you create at essexny.us/contact, facebook.com/essexny, and twitter.com/essexny. We can't wait to see your doodles!

"The aspects of things that are most important for us are hidden because of their simplicity and familiarity. (One is unable to notice something— because it is always before one's eyes.)"

~ Ludwig Wittgenstein, *Philosophical Investigations*

Georgian Architecture

Georgian architecture is one of the earliest building styles visible in Essex. Popular in 18th century England (and drawing upon classical Roman designs celebrated by the Italian Renaissance), Georgian architecture was widely adopted in Colonial America.

"Georgian architecture respected the scale of both the individual and the community." ~ Stephen Gardiner

Common Georgian architecture features:

- One- or two-story, rectangular construction
- Symmetrical five-bay façade
- Center entrance with paneled front door
- Decoration (entablature) over front door
- Pilasters or columns flank front door
- Aligned windows (grid pattern)
- Double-hung sash windows

- Typically windows are small six-over-six panes with thick muntins and/or larger twelve-over-twelve panes
- Decorated cornice moldings (often dentil)
- Paired chimneys (one on each end of home)
- Medium pitched (hipped or gambrel) roof
- Raised foundation

Essex buildings exhibiting Georgian details:

- Dower House
- Ralph Hascall House
- Rosslyn (also Federal and Greek Revival elements)

TRY This! Doodle typically Georgian style architectural details from one of the three buildings listed. Or try to identify Georgian elements from another building. (Hint: Consider the street view of the oldest remaining schoolhouse in Essex.)

Federal Architecture

Many historians consider Federal architecture a refinement of its Georgian antecedents, incorporating greater delicacy and lightness. Prevalent throughout the newly independent colonies, Federal architecture is understated but often incorporates curved lines and decorative embellishments.

Hickory Hill, considered the most prominent example of the Federal architecture style in Essex, exhibits a typical five-bay Federal façade with pairs of windows to either side of a central entrance.

Common Federal architecture features:

- Two-story, rectangular construction
- Symmetrical five-bay façade
- Center entrance with paneled front door
- Semicircular fanlight over front door

- Narrow side lights flank front door
- Decorative crown or roof over front door
- Columns with elaborate capitals
- Palladian window or elliptical windows
- Aligned windows (grid pattern)
- Double-hung sash windows
- Twelve-over-tweleve or twelve-over-eight panes with thin muntins
- Louvered shutters
- Embellished cornice moldings
- Decorative swags, garlands and/or fluting
- Low-hipped or flat roof with balustrade
- Raised foundation

Essex buildings exhibiting Federal details:

- Hickory Hill (also later Greek Revival elements)
- Rosslyn (also Georgian and Greek Revival elements)
- John Gould House (also Greek Revival elements)

Doodle an Essex building with 3 or more Federal elements listed above. Want an extra challenge? Doodle a building other than Hickory Hill.

Greek Revival Architecture

Greek Revival architecture swept our recently independent nation in the first half of the 19th century. Idealized Grecian designs (such as the classic temple form of the Parthenon) popularized in books by Asher Benjamin transformed residential and commercial buildings.

Common Greek Revival architecture features:

- Gable-front roof (perpendicular to the street)
- Heavy entablature and cornice
- Symmetrical façade (often with off-center entrance)
- Doric, Ionic, or Corinthian columns

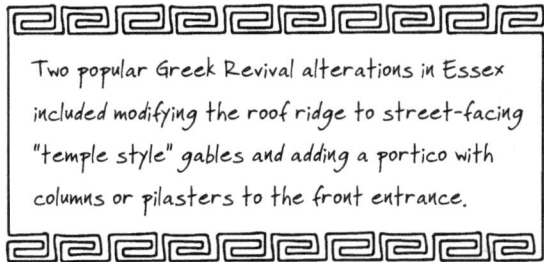

Two popular Greek Revival alterations in Essex included modifying the roof ridge to street-facing "temple style" gables and adding a portico with columns or pilasters to the front entrance.

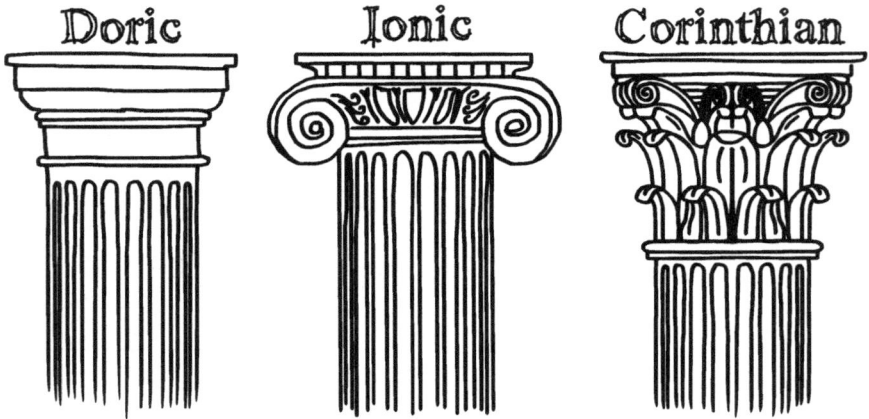

Doric   Ionic   Corinthian

- Narrow side lights flank front door
- Double-hung sash windows (six over six panes)
- Gable or hipped roof of low pitch
- Low-hipped or gambrel) roof
- Entry porch or full-width porch with prominent columns
- Chimneys are not prominent

Essex buildings exhibiting Greek Revival details:

- Greystone
- Cyrus Stafford House
- Block House Farm
- Essex Inn (Greek Revival additions: porch-colonnade)

Take a photograph of a Federal
building and "doodlebomb" it with
Greek Revival elements from the
list above. It's a doodle "makeover"!

Victorian Architecture

Victorian architecture is a broad and diverse classification with many style subsets, only a few of which were utilized in Essex, including the Gothic Revival, Italianate, Queen Anne, and Second Empire styles. If you take a walk through Essex you will notice some steep roofs, bay windows, and intricate iron fences all inspired by the Victorian era. However, few new homes were built in Essex during that era, and the majority of Victorian design elements were merely modifications to existing buildings. Yet, there are some examples of completely Victorian buildings to be seen.

An example of the Italianate style, the Noble Clemons House stands in marked contrast to other prominent historic homes in the village of Essex with its nearly-flat roof, wide eaves, and massive brackets, likening it to an Italian villa.

Common Victorian architecture features:

- Bay windows
- Steeply pitched roofs
- Bracketed cornices
- Detailed iron fences
- Intricately designed interior and exterior hardware and ornamentation
- Ornamental fireplaces
- Slender chimneys for iron stoves or smaller coal-burning fireplaces

Essex buildings exhibiting Victorian details:

- Harmon Noble Schoolhouse (Gothic Revival & Italianate)
- Rosslyn Boathouse (Eastlake Design, facet of the Queen Anne style)
- Noble Clemons House (Italianate)
- Essex Community Church (Italianate)
- St. John's Episcopal Church (Gothic Revival)

Doodle
Dare U

Combine Victorian architectural elements from two or more Essex buildings to create a brand new building.

1. Dower House

The northernmost residence (furthest from the ferry dock) on Merchant Row, this white clapboard house with red shutters was constructed between the late 1780s and the turn of the

century and is the oldest documented home in the Essex Village Historic District.

The five-bay façade and gambrel roof still reveal the residence's 18th century pedigree despite generations of renovations and alterations.

The two-story wood frame residence is predominantly Georgian in style. The gable ends of the gambrel roof are situated perpendicular to Lake Shore Road, orienting the eastern façade toward the lake.

A central entryway flanked by sidelights establishes a sense of balance that is emphasized with a pair of first story windows on either side of the entrance, as well as symmetrical basement windows and chimneys situated at the north and south end of the original house.

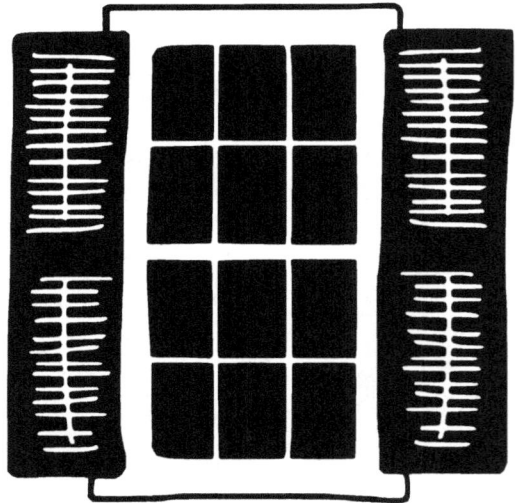

Dormers and north and south wings were added later (Colonial Revival Style) but sensitively preserve the proportion and balance that distinguish Dower House. Doodle the residence without additions as it might have appeared in the late 1700s.

2. Wright's Inn

Essex Town Hall is located in one of the oldest enduring architectural structures in Essex. Situated at the southwest corner of Main Street and NYS Route 22, this long, narrow wood-frame building was constructed in two phases.

Daniel Ross constructed the southern half for use as an inn and tavern circa 1790, and the original five-bay, central entryway typical of Georgian style architecture is still discernible today. (Although the portico is not original, it is a faithful recreation.)

First story windows with original carved wooden lintels are replicas of

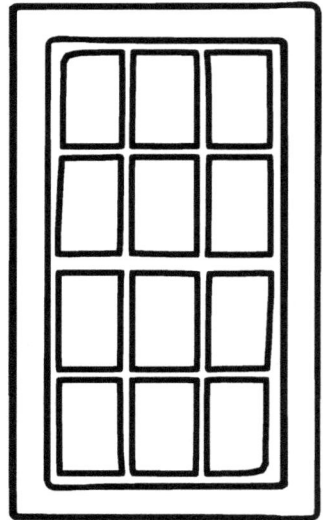

the 1840s sash found hung on the rear façade. (Original sash was probably twelve-over-twelve and/or nine-over-six). 1870s era photographs show that original "quoins" made of wood had been applied along the corners of the façade also of the Georgian style.

General Daniel Wright purchased the building in 1798 and added the northern half of the building in the early 19th century.

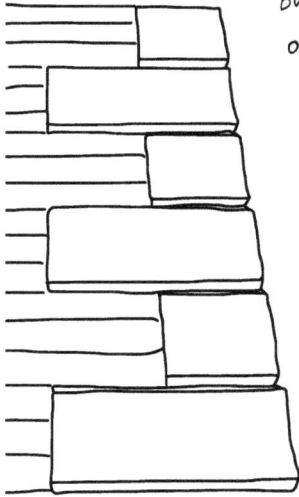

One of several local inns thriving as Essex prospered, Wright's Inn was acquired by Hiram Fancher who, in the 1830s, added a rear ell, upgraded it with a two story porch facing Main Street similar to the one still visible at the Essex Inn to the south, and by 1846 built the three bay addition now present on the north of the structure. Paying attention to the dressed limestone foundation stones one can see this division.

In the very early 1900s a "double decker" front porch was added in the

31

"Adirondack" style as Essex adapted to tourism, however it was later removed.

Over the years the building's name and function evolved, but a shrinking population and economy in the latter half of the 20th century nearly brought an end to the historic inn and tavern. In 1969 Wright's Inn was donated to the Town of Essex, and although demolition plans were considered in the 1970s, the cooperation, persistence and generosity of many saved the building and repurposed Wright's Inn for civic use as well as catalyzed the creation of the Essex Community Heritage Organization (now Historic Essex).

Doodle the Wright's Inn during its heyday as an inn and tavern.

CRAYON

On the next page doodle
an architectural map of
Essex. You decide what
does or doesn't get included. Check out www.essexny.
us/map for an interactive
Essex map and a printable
PDF... Use the space
on this page to practice
what to include in your map.

Doodle Your Own Essex Map

Map of Essex

3. Ralph Hascall House

    The Ralph Hascall House was built sometime between 1800 and 1810 in a five-bay, hipped roof, Georgian style for an Essex lawyer and New York State Senator. It is one of the few examples of this style of architecture in Essex, and its unaligned placement and lower grade to the street suggests it was built before Main Street was laid out. Despite many alterations over the years, this centrally located residence

has been painstakingly restored to near-original condition and architectural style.

Mid nineteenth century renovations concealed the original hip roof beneath a steeper, eave front gable roof, similar to many others in the Essex Village Historic District. The front façade's classical and neoclassical elements were also obscured by several generations of additions.

A first story porch extending the full width of the home was added circa 1870, and a second story sleeping porch or "cure porch" (used for treating tuberculosis patients) was added shortly after 1908 by a resident physician. The home's original Palladian window was repurposed into a door to access the upper porch, the windows on either side of the front entrance had been replaced with French doors, and an oriel window was added.

But the Essex Community Heritage Organization (now Historic Essex) undertook a dramatic restoration of the Ralph Hascall House in the 1980s, returning the roof and Main Street façade to their appearance at the dawn of the 19th century. This

project sparked debate in the preservation community over whether to preserve enough layers to show what happened to the building over time, or to strip away those later details to showcase its original Georgian details. In the end the rarity of Georgian style elsewhere in Essex swayed the decision to restore versus preserve.

The original hip roof, which remained partially intact within the attic space beneath the replacement gable roof, was uncovered and restored. The Georgian entrance with original fanlight is once again prominent after the porches were removed, and the Main Street facade was completely restored by replicating two original twelve-over-twelve double-hung sash windows that remained on the southern side of the house. Today this house serves as a reference point when comparing Essex's original Georgian style with more prevalent, later styles exhibited elsewhere.

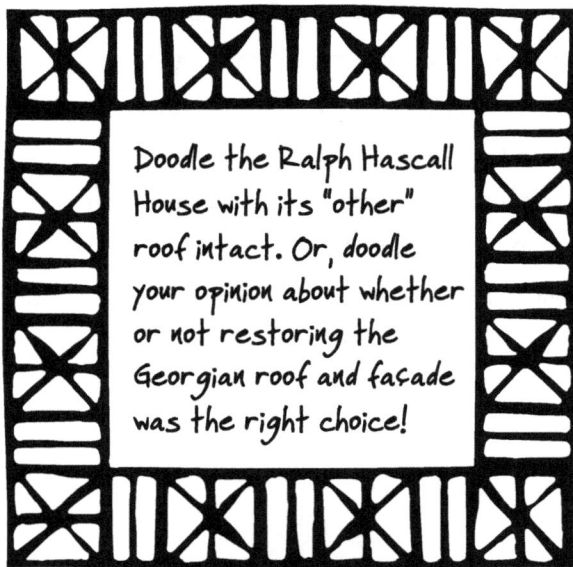

Doodle the Ralph Hascall House with its "other" roof intact. Or, doodle your opinion about whether or not restoring the Georgian roof and façade was the right choice!

Doodle Street View

Imagine that several of your favorite Essex buildings
are located side-by-side. Doodle the street view...

4. Old Essex Firehouse

The Old Essex Firehouse, prominently situated at the intersection of Rte 22 and Main Street, is the southernmost of three adjacent waterfront commercial buildings constructed of blue-gray limestone (also known as Chazy limestone and Essex bluestone).

Constructed shortly after 1800, the original limestone façade was concealed circa 1835 when the two-story wooden porch and the pediment with sunburst adornment were added.

The building was originally occupied by a dry goods shop and women's hat maker (millinery). In 1812 Henry H. Ross expanded the building for use as his law office.

In the early 1900s the building housed a telephone exchange in the second story and Farm Bureau organization offices. In 1931 it was converted into a station for the Essex Volunteer Fire Department. The basement was filled with sand and a cement floor was poured to withstand the weight of the fire trucks.

In 1999 the town sold the property and it was rehabilitated into gallery space, and the second story was converted into a private apartment.

Three overhead garage doors were replaced along the front façade with fixed sash windows and a rear porch overlooking Lake Champlain was added.

This emblematic commercial building housed the Adirondack Art Association's seasonal gallery until the summer of 2013.

The sunburst motif, popular in Greek Revival buildings throughout the Champlain Valley, has become emblematic of the Essex Village Historic District and has influenced much local design and iconography. Create an abstract doodle inspired by the sunburst from the Old Essex Firehouse.

Doodle Your Favorite Building

Doodle your favorite Essex building that is NOT included in this book.

5. Noble Warehouse

Located just south of the Essex ferry dock, this warehouse and adjoining wharf were originally built by Ransom Noble circa 1810 to facilitate maritime commerce. The simple but practical limestone building's form was dictated by its function. Simple windows illuminated the interior with natural light, and large loading bays facing Lake Champlain provided efficient cargo access.

The building was later converted to house the W.G. Lyons general store downstairs and a shirt factory upstairs. In the 1920s, it was transformed into a concert hall and summer stock theater by Maud Noble who renamed it Harlan Hall in honor of her late husband U.S. Supreme Court Justice John Marshall Harlan.

As the building's function evolved so too did its architecture and design. A stage and balcony were added to the interior to accommodate performers and audience. Colonial Revival elements were later added; a neoclassical entrance was installed to welcome patrons into the concert hall, and Palladian windows were installed to embellish the warehouse's previously sparse, utilitarian west and east facades.

Another significant alteration to the building's exterior is the stairway enclosure on the southern end of the building. Clapboard siding concealed the limestone facade, windows were installed diagonally in keeping with the stairway within, and the entrance was ornamented with a fanlight and keystone-arched door surround.

Over the years the former Noble Warehouse has also housed a movie theater and residential apartments before Cornelia Hand Baird, a descendant of the Noble family, donated the building to the Masons on July 19, 1944. Today the building remains a Masonic Lodge (Iroquois Lodge

#715 Free and Accepted Masons) and the summer home of Essex Theatre Company productions.

Create a doodle that combines some of the Noble Warehouse's architectural details and its many uses over the years.

6. W.D. Ross Store

Located across Main Street from the Essex Community Church, the W.D. Ross Store was built for William D. Ross circa 1810 to serve as a warehouse and store and also as a law office.

Constructed of locally quarried limestone, this commercial building exhibits very little style. It is a utilitarian building with typical detailing, small-paned windows, a molded cornice at the eaves, and probably had a solid, 6-panel or multi-panel wooden door originally. Its symmetry has been attributed to the Greek Revival style, although some would disagree and say that the building draws that symmetry from Federal origins. What do you think?

Greek Revival?

The second and third story freight doors, an interior freight elevator and robust construction materials throughout offer testament to the shipping and mercantile demands placed upon this sturdy Main Street annex for the Ross family's bustling wharf and dock house.

As with many Essex buildings, the W.D. Ross Store was altered often over the centuries. The storefront and wood frame addition on the north side of the warehouse were added to the original structure, and the addition's roof, which extended the building's existing roofline, was subsequently replaced with the current single story roof.

F.H.SHERMAN

Observe, imagine, and wonder. And then doodle
the building's past, present, and future. (Or
doodle something that you spy through the
window...)

7. Essex Inn

The Essex Inn is almost as old as the town in which it has thrived for two centuries, and is the oldest working inn still surviving. Since the early 19th century when Essex was growing rapidly, the Essex Inn has been a social hub for merchants, visitors and residents.

The Essex Inn was built in stages. The southern portion was constructed circa 1810 in Federal style with a five-bay façade parallel to the street and triangular gable roof ends. The inn was expanded circa 1829 and joined with a similar framed building situated to its north, creating a close resemblance to Wright's Inn.

The dominant Greek Revival colonnade was added around 1835, but the railing on the first story of the porch was not added until much later. Originally the inn had twelve-over-twelve sash in the windows, but it was changed to six-over-six when the colonnade was added.

What would the Essex Inn look like if the street view façade had been modified with Victorian embellishments instead of the Greek Revival colonnade?

8. Crystal Spring Farm

Crystal Spring Farm is a Federal style farmhouse on the northern outskirts of the village that is undergoing a substantial rehabilitation after many years neglected.

Originally constructed circa 1811, this handsome but un-assuming residence exhibits characteristic Federal elements including a symmetrical five-bay facade with center entrance; grid-pattern, double-hung sash windows; louvered shutters; and a pair of brick chimneys that mirror each other from the north and south ends of the roof.

A modestly proportioned portico overhangs the front door with two understated columns and low balusters stretching between the columns and the house. Behind the main building, a perpendicular wing (or ell) extends westward with a south-facing porch overlooking the lawn and fields (visible from the sidewalk).

Early Essex County historian Albert Hayward (1903-1982) lived in this house for many years, hence the home sometimes being known as the Hayward House. Hayward preserved records of his research and correspondence, and many of those were donated to the Paine Memorial Library in Willsboro following his death.

Can you transform Crystal Spring Farm into a Victorian style building? Look across the street at Wilder House for inspiration.

9. Greystone Cottage

Long before Greystone Cottage was converted into a municipal repository of books, the handsome stone building adjacent to the Essex-Charlotte ferry dock was part of Ransom Noble's thriving mercantile business.

Noble established a tannery in the early 19th century beside the stream, now called Library Brook, directly west of the building. He constructed the stone building between 1801 and 1818 to sell merchandise produced in his tannery and shoe factory located behind the building. Later it became the H. and B. Noble General Store.

Constructed of native limestone, the exterior of the building displays little ornamentation. As one of four structures comprising the commercial core around Essex's old ferry dock (including the Old Firehouse, W.D. Ross Store, and Noble Warehouse) its design and architecture is simple and utilitarian without elaborate decoration.

Only the splayed lintels over windows and the twelve-over-eight sash in the upper windows originate from the building's initial design. The two matching balconies and diamond pane windows on the first floor were added in late 1800s and dressed up the façade.

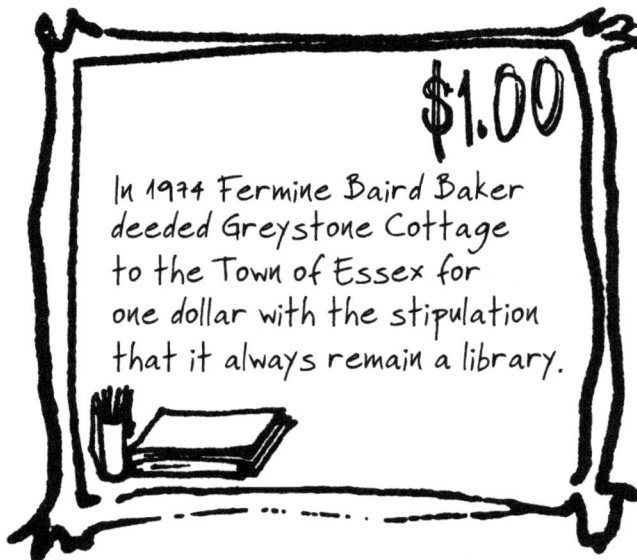

$1.00

In 1974 Fermine Baird Baker deeded Greystone Cottage to the Town of Essex for one dollar with the stipulation that it always remain a library.

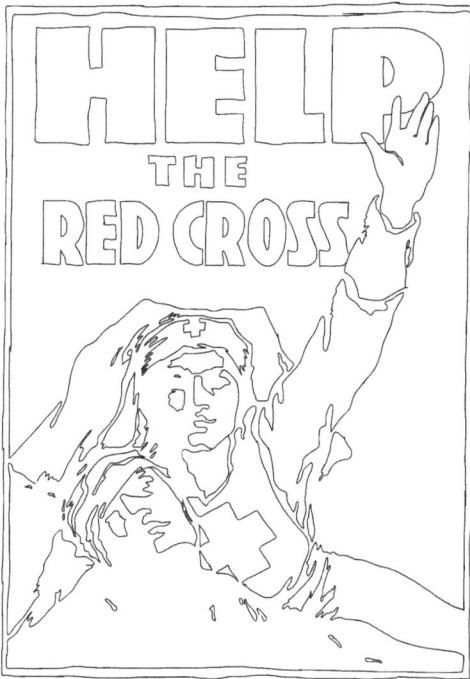

After the building ceased to be used commercially, Adeline Noble used the store space to house a private library. Eventually, a "provisional" charter was granted and the town accepted the public Essex Free Library in 1899. It was in 1906 that the library received "absolute" charter.

During World War I and World War II Greystone Cottage was used by the Red Cross.

In 1998, the library received a grant that allowed the exterior and interior of the library to be restored by ECHO and the library board; photographs of the original designs were studied to make the restoration as historically accurate as possible.

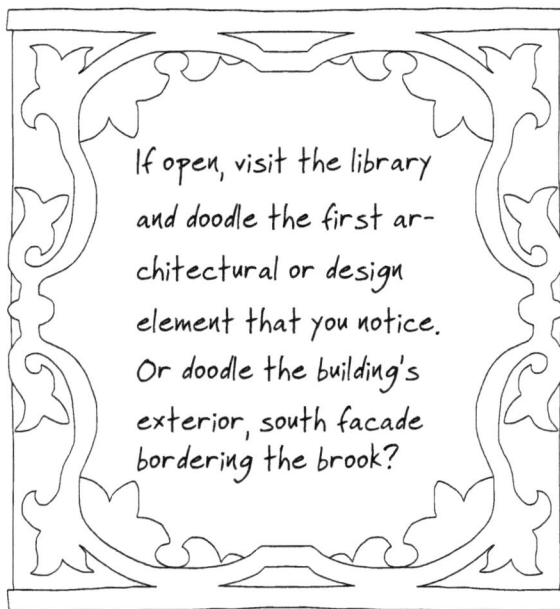

If open, visit the library and doodle the first architectural or design element that you notice. Or doodle the building's exterior, south facade bordering the brook?

Doodle Artifact

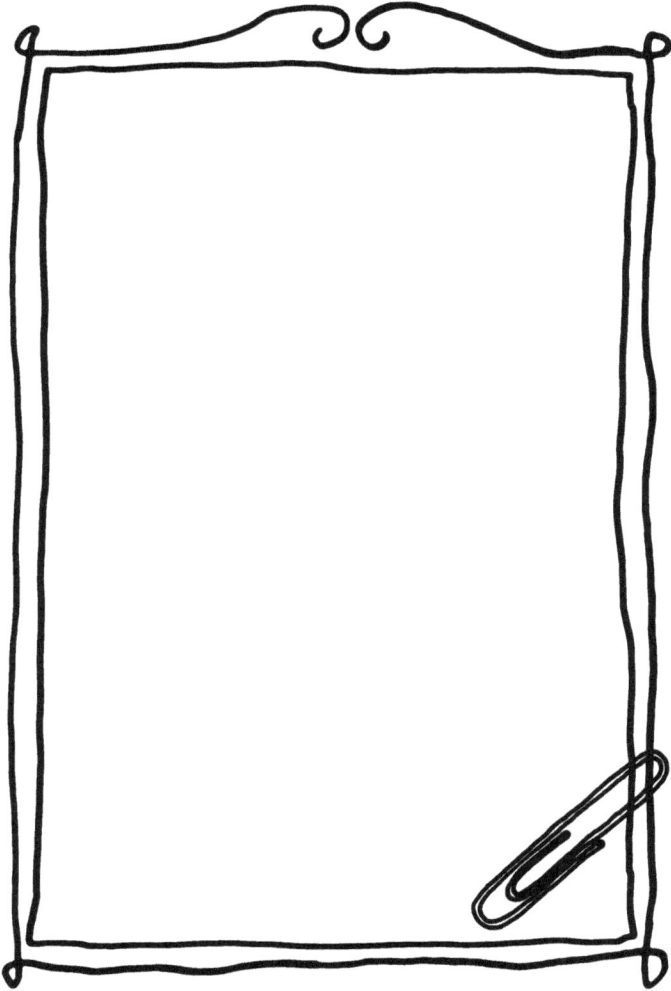

Find and attach an Essex artifact to this page (i.e. a photo, business card, brochure, postcard, flyer, etc.) Doodle the building where you acquired it...

10. John Gould House

In 1817 John Gould began purchasing and combining land parcels just south of Essex's town center to build a home. By the time construction of his residence was completed (circa 1833) on the west side of Main Street he owned nearly the entire block.

"John Gould House contains classical elements in the refined taste of the Greek Revival style!"
~ David Hislop

The five-bay façade and plan of the main limestone residence is of the more conservative Federal style, but Greek Revival embellishments are incorporated. The six-over-six windows and elaborate portico at the entrance are the obvious features of the Greek Revival style. What else do you see?

The columned entrance portico and cut gray limestone exterior lend the John Gould House a similar (if slightly more modest) resemblance to Greystone that was constructed two decades later. Perhaps the John Gould House served as inspiration for Greystone?

A Gothic Revival gazebo on the grounds is the only reminder of the properties once grand gardens.

The Palmer Havens Gardens were large, formal Victorian ornamental gardens that once attracted visitors to the grounds of the John Gould House. Doodle what you think they looked like.

11. Old Brick Schoolhouse

The Old Brick Schoolhouse, located on Elm Street between Elm Street and Route 22, marks the site of the first school in Essex. Part of the original structure (built in 1787) may have been incorporated into the current building when it was rebuilt in 1818 as a one-room schoolhouse.

The shipping industry was soon booming in Essex necessitating a larger school. A second room was

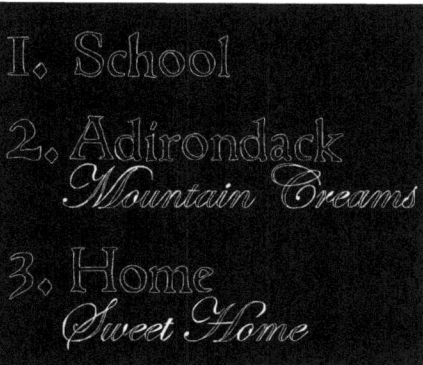

1. School

2. Adirondack
   Mountain Creams

3. Home
   Sweet Home

added in 1836 to accommodate the growing student body, effectively doubling the classroom space. This schoolhouse served Essex residents until the Union School was constructed in 1867. Later, the building was used as a candy factory for John Bird Burnham's Adirondack Mountain Creams in the early 1900s, and then in the early 1970s it was renovated into a residential home.

The simple brick building has minimal embellishment. The belfry was originally centered on the one-room building's roof, but when the addition was made it was shifted to remain at the center of the now longer building.

Original wooden shutters with hand-crafted 18th century nails and hinges still remain on the twelve-over twelve sash windows. A door is located in the center of the long street-facing façade with a rectangular multi-paned transom window above the doorway. On the southern side two more doors are located, originally used as separate boys' and girls' entrances, each doorway also has a transom window above but of more simple design.

Doodle the bell tower.
Or doodle some of the
building's many uses.

12. Hickory Hill

In 1822, Henry Howard Ross built Hickory Hill atop a ridge overlooking Essex village and Lake Champlain. Situated at the intersection of Elm and Church Street and modeled on upon a Federal home in Salem, New York, this five-bay, two-and-a-half-story, brick residence exhibits the restrained elegance characteristic of Federal style architecture.

Hickory Hill's stately eastern façade exhibits a delicate Palladian window, intricately ornamented cornices, splayed marble lintels above the windows, and a central portico supported by tall, thin Roman Doric columns that greet visitors as they ascend a long flight of limestone steps. Narrow sidelights and pilasters that resemble the outward pillars frame the original six-panel door, and it is crowned with a delicate leaded-glass fanlight.

The back of the home still retains the original twelve-over-twelve sash windows. Casement windows were added in the late 19th century.

In 1845 H.H. Ross added to the north side of Hickory Hill to accommodate his law offices, the design reflecting an architectural shift from Federal to Greek Revival influences. The frieze with carved wave motif and the more prominent columns and decorations on the home's east entrance are telltale Greek Revival elements.

Incorporate the carved wave motif from the Greek Revival frieze into a doodle. Or doodle several Federal and Greek Revival elements visible from the street.

13. Rosslyn

Rosslyn, the second oldest home on Merchant Row (circa 1820), is located just south of Dower House. This historic home was built by William D. Ross for his bride Mary Ann Gould.

Primarily Federal in style, Rosslyn also exhibits elements of Georgian and Greek Revival architecture. The central entryway of the five-bay façade is flanked by sidelight windows placed symmetrically on both sides of the entrance and an elegant fanlight sits above the doorway. Four tall, slender chimneys rise from the roofline.

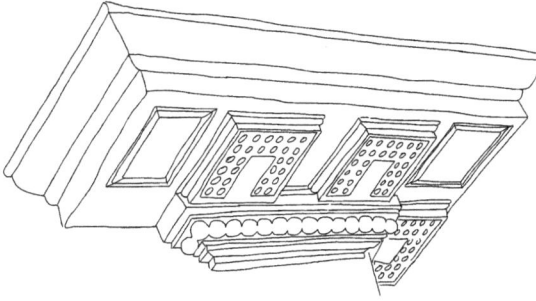

The "dentillated" Doric cornice is copied from *The American Builder's Companion* an 1826 pattern book by Boston architect Asher Benjamin.

Early in the 20th century Rosslyn was converted into the Sherwood Inn, and the rear service wing (kitchen, pantry, servants' quarters, etc.) was repurposed to accommodate guest lodging, restaurant and tavern. By the late 1950s or early 1960s the Sherwood Inn had ceased operation. Part of the rear wing was demolished and the rest was adapted to residential use.

Expansive lawns, locally quarried stone walls, and the alignment (and spacing) of Rosslyn's outbuildings contribute to the balanced composition and proportions of this property. Limestone seawalls, ruins of a waterfront wharf (still visible during low water), and a whimsical boathouse reveal the property's maritime heritage and decades of use as The Sherwood Inn, a popular vacation destination.

GEORGIAN ✛ FEDERAL ✛
✛   GREEK REVIVAL
GREEK REVIVAL

Can you identify &
DOODLE
some of Rosslyn's
Georgian, Federal &
Greek Revival details?

✛
✛ GEORGIAN ✛ FEDERAL ✛

Doodle Game

Me

You

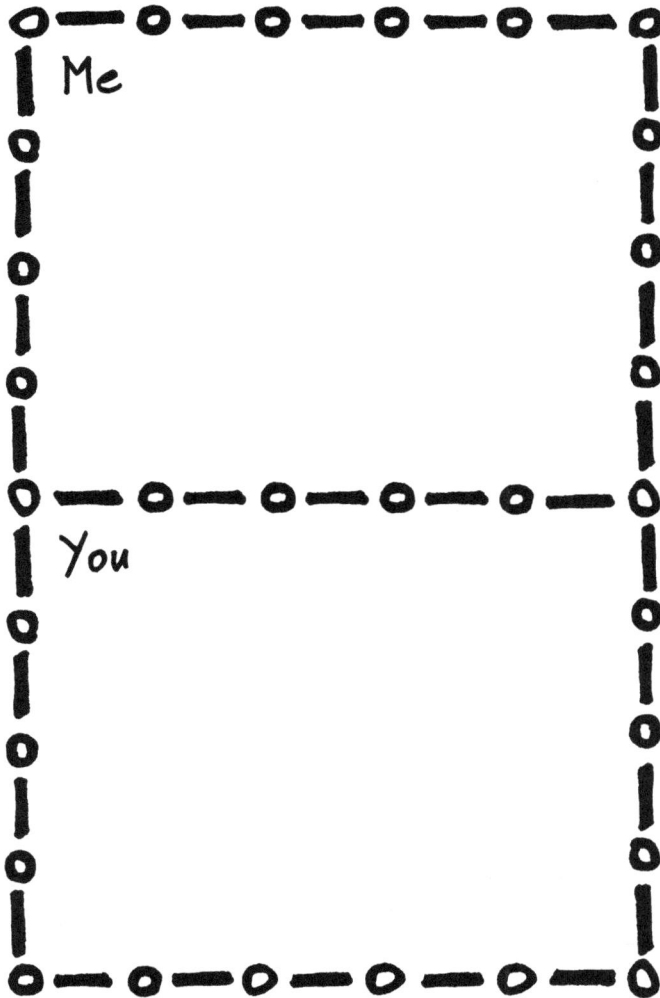

Doodle an Essex building, and ask a friend to guess which building it is. Then let you friend doodle, and try to identify their doodle.

14. Billings Stone Cottage

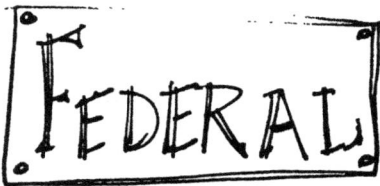

FEDERAL

Located on the south-west corner of School Street and Elm Street, Billings Stone Cottage is a Federal period cottage that was constructed by stonemason P.P. Billings (who moved to Essex after working on the Champlain Canal) using gray limestone quarried immediately behind the house.

The cottage was built (circa 1828) on land purchased by wealthy Essex merchants Ransom and Harmon Noble. Their descendants owned and maintained it for over 100 years, often using it as a tenant house.

Simple construction and meticulous stonework indicate the solidity and permanence of this otherwise understated building. The exterior walls expose the rectangular and square stones used to construct the building on the sides and front, while the back is composed of rubble stone.

The twelve-over-twelve sash windows and front door with sidelights add a little lightness to this Federal cottage.

Doodle the Billings Stone Cottage
with elaborate Federal details.
Or, gussy it up with
Greek Revival embellishments.
Have a friend try too,
and then compare your doodles!

15. Dr. Samuel Shumway House

The stone Dr. Samuel Shumway House was built in the stately Federal style in the early 1800s. However, it is not solely that style but has some Greek Revival architectural influences; it is a unique home that is simply "Essex."

Because Shumway House is situated at the corner of two streets it displays two dominant facades. The Church Street facade exhibits a classic Federal style entrance decorated by a flattened stonework arch along the top, a semi-elliptical louvered fanlight, and narrow sidelights along either side of the doorway.

The Elm Street facade is significantly longer and includes an off-center entrance with the doorway sheltered beneath a small portico that was added in the late 1800s. The pair of gabled dormers that jut out of the roof on west and east sides of the house were added at a later date.

Doodle the Dr. Samuel Shumway House while sitting or standing on Church Street. Then doodle it from Elm Street. Doodle as many architectural details as you can.

16. Harmon Noble House

The Harmon Noble House was built on Merchant Row in 1835 by Ransom Noble's son, Harmon. Referred to also as Sunnyside or the Noble-Schreiber House, this understated brick residence commands a panoramic view of Lake Champlain and Vermont's Green Mountains.

The Harmon Noble House blends a Federal plan (five-bay façade with central entryway) with Greek Revival embellishments (entryway portico with Greek key on all three sides of the architrave) resulting in a handsome but understated balance.

Like Greystone and Rosslyn, the Harmon Noble House includes multiple chimneys, a reminder of the importance of fireplaces to

heat a home in the 19th century. However, by the time this home was built it's likely that the chimneys would be connected to iron stoves or smaller fireplaces with stove inserts.

The cast iron fence dates from the 1860s and matches the fence in front of Greystone (next door), which was built by Harmon Noble's brother, Belden.

Note: The octagonal one-room schoolhouse (resembling a decorative garden gazebo) is featured separately toward the end of this handbook. Check it out!

Transform the Harmon Noble House into a Victorian house with as many embellishments as possible.

17. St. John's Episcopal Church

Episcopal services were originally held in the small Ross family schoolhouse at Hickory Hill, which was constructed around 1835. In 1854 Henry H. Ross leased the building to the congregation and it was officially converted into an Episcopal church.

"In 1877, the church purchased the building and lot, removed the old building to its present site, and reconstructed it in its present form, using designs by the Reverend John Henry Hopkins" (Belden Noble Memorial Library, *Essex, New York: An Early History*).

St. John's Episcopal Church, situated at the southeast corner of Church and Elm Streets, was renovated with Gothic architectural elements including visible buttresses, a whimsical bell cote, and arched stained glass windows.

The buttresses were not structurally necessary, but were likely added to resemble the elaborate Gothic churches in Europe. (Note: The west wing was added in 1984 to serve as a parish hall.)

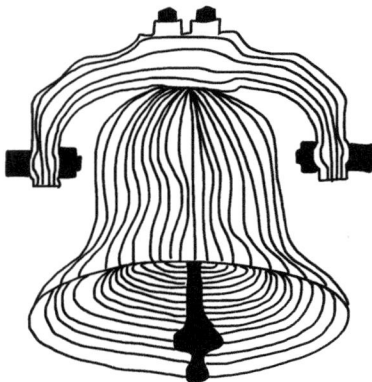

A bell cote is a structure or framework for hanging bells when there is no belfry...

The bell atop the church was salvaged from the lake steamer, *Champlain II*, which ran aground between Westport and Essex in 1875. Other details of interest are the arched stained glass windows on the south facade that were crafted by Taber Sears of New York, circa 1910 ("Essex: An Architectural Guide").

Doodle the church with Greek Revival embellishments.
Or, if you feel nautical, doodle the *Champlain II*.

Aha! Moment

Doodle an SX architecture "Aha! moment" (aka "Eureka effect", insight, epiphany) that you've experienced.

18. Block House Farm

Block House Farm (circa 1836) is located near the northern limit of the village. It is the only instance of fully developed Greek Revival temple style architecture in Essex. On the street-facing façade four Doric columns support a large pediment inset with a sunburst fanlight.

Side dormers (a Colonial Revival element) protrude from the roof line on the north and south sides (probably added to provide more usable attic space sometime in the 20th century) deviate from the classic Greek temple form but help chronicle the home's evolution.

Block House Farm draws its name from an eighteenth century blockhouse that served as a combination of courthouse, jail and fort. Today an historical marker indicates the former location of the blockhouse slightly south of the residence. Allegedly, timbers from the original blockhouse were recycled for construction of the barn that still stands on the Block House Farm property.

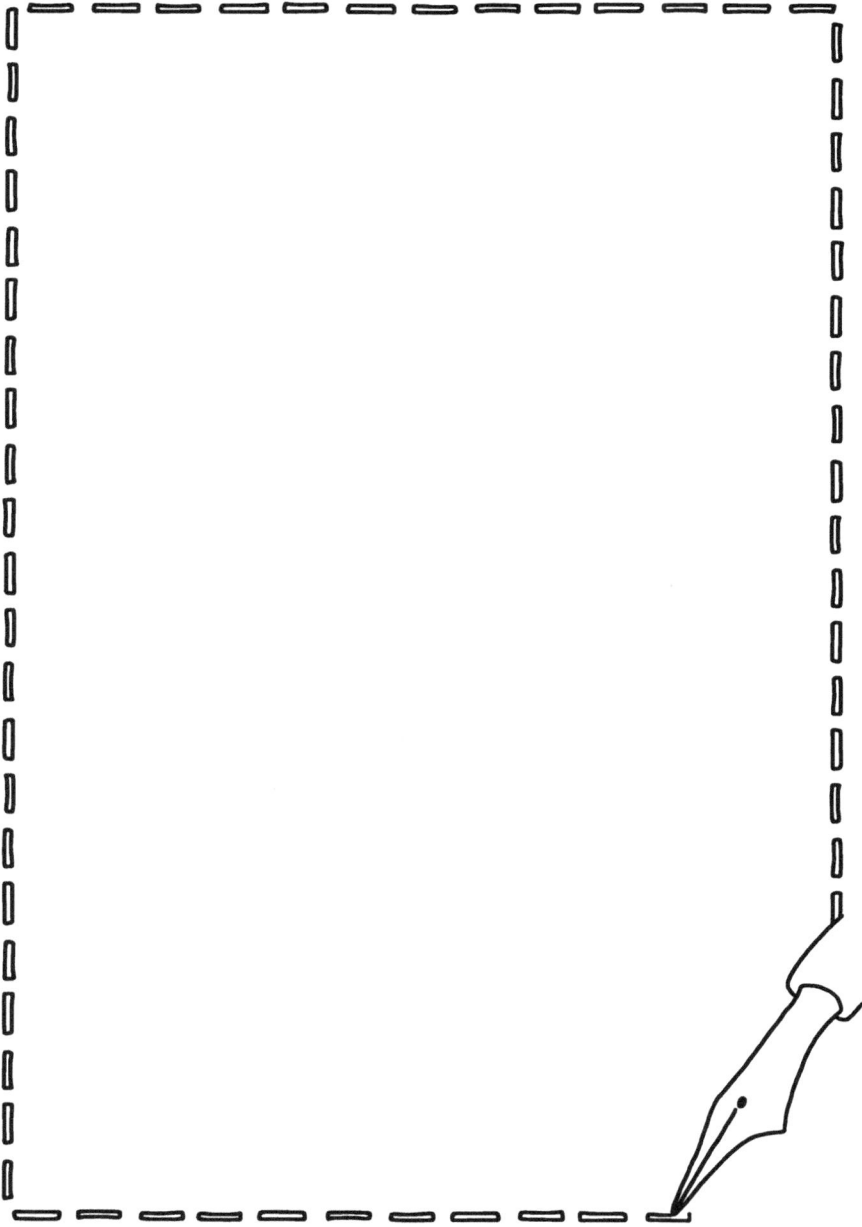

Imagine the historic block house... Now, doodle it!

19. Edwards Store

Located at the corner of School Street and Main Street, the Edwards Store was built (circa 1836) by tailor Henry Edwards.

This brick Greek Revival building (street-facing, three-bay gable) was subsequently embellished with Victorian details including

Carpenter Gothic verge-boards (the lacy decoration along the eaves) and two bay windows. The Edwards Store still retains the original six-over-six light sash windows.

The small door located in the peak of the front gable was originally equipped with a block and tackle pulley system that was used to load supplies into the loft. Perhaps the stairway inside was inadequate to easily carry big or heavy loads up to the second floor, or maybe it was simply more efficient to use the outdoor pulley system?

Over the years many owners and businesses have passed through the Edwards Store (aka the Edwards Brick Store). Originally used as a men's haberdashery (clothing store), it has since been occupied by several retail stores and even served as the village liquor store. If you look under the bay windows you may be able to make out some very faded advertising from its time as a shoe store. It is currently used as a seasonal rental residence.

Imagine visiting Edwards Store the year it opened. Doodle yourself or a friend getting outfitted with period clothing and other accessories...

20. Old Stone Church

The Old Stone Church, located on Church Street between Main and Elm Streets, is the oldest church that remains standing in the village; however, it no longer serves as a church. The Methodist Episcopal Church was organized on January 12, 1835, and this building was constructed the following year with improvements made to the church in 1876 and 1884.

The limestone church provides a simple expression of the Gothic Revival style. The lancet arch windows are perhaps the most recognizable Gothic feature on the exterior. The stonework around these windows is indicative of very fine original craftsmanship, although the colorful stained glass in the windows is a nineteenth-century alteration.

Church services discontinued at the Old Stone Church in 1922 when the town's Methodist Episcopal, Baptist and Presbyterian congregations merged into the Federated Church (or what is today known as the Essex Community Church).

The bell tower and steeple that adorned this church roof were removed half a century ago. Can you doodle the church with the bell tower and steeple restored?

21. Old Brick Store

The Old Brick Store is a practical Greek Revival commercial building located at the corner of Main and School Streets
that was built around 1840.

Greek Revival

Its overall architectural design is simple, but the building exhibits a few notable details. Dressed stone lintels (and sills) adorn the two upper windows, and the brick cornice is corbeled to imitate dentils. The storefront is adorned with pilasters which match the paneled door surround.

"Dentils" are small, rectangular blocks used to decorate the cornice. The word is derived from their resemblance to teeth!

ESSEX

The original three-bay storefront façade offers tribute to Essex's mid-nineteenth-century commercial activity. Many businesses have operated here over the years including Essex Market (c. 1905) and Huston's (c. 1980).

Can you doodle the Old Brick Store as it might have appeared when business was booming? Perhaps a street view with display tables, heaps of fresh produce, and customers shopping? Or maybe a glimpse inside, with shelves and counters full of merchandise?

22. Edwards House

The Edwards House adjoins the Edwards Store which was built by Henry Edwards prior to the residence. Completed circa 1841 in the Greek Revival style, this two-story brick building employs a Greek Revival "temple-form central block (cella) with flanking one-storey subsidiary wings" ("Essex: An Architectural Guide"). The cornice on the central block protrudes, highlighting the restrained-but-stately form and lines of the roof.

The wings were altered at some point, most likely to add a full second floor. The subsidiary wings' original roofs were replaced with slate-covered gambrel roofs, Colonial Revival in style, that remain today.

Two original details that continue to lend elegance to the Main Street façade of the Edwards House are the semi-elliptical fanlight and the embellished entrance. The fanlight conspicuously crowns the temple end, echoing the familiar Essex sunburst motif. The entryway is covered by a portico with two square columns that support a small roof wrapped in crown molding. The entrance is flanked by two pairs of Greek key pilasters, a frieze with a carved motif above the door and windows, and elegant paneling below the windows.

Imagine the Edwards House as it was originally constructed (prior to the gambrel roofs). Can you doodle what the building may have looked like?

Essex Limestone

Many historic buildings in Essex were constructed with locally quarried limestone *officially* called "Middlebury and Chazy Limestone" (or simply "Chazy Limestone") but known to residents and visitors as "Essex limestone" (also "Essex bluestone / blue-gray limestone / blue-tinted limestone / etc.") This once abundant building material can be found in most Essex foundations, and eleven of the buildings featured in this book are primarily built with it. How many can you locate and micro-doodle (small, quick thumbnail images) in the space above?

23. Cyrus Stafford House

This Greek Revival residence located on the south side of Route 22 between Main and Elm Streets was built in 1847 for Cyrus Stafford, an Essex merchant.

Sitting prominently in the heart of the historic village, the house combines construction materials (brick, wood, and local limestone) prevalent in many of Essex's historical properties. The carving on the steps

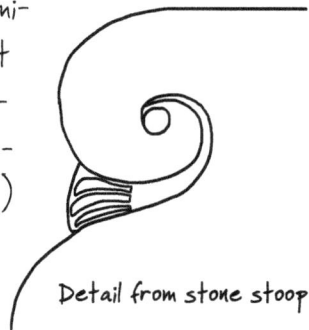

Detail from stone stoop

is meant to imitate pre-historic mollusks found in the Chazy lime-stone itself.

The street-facing gable end with embellished roof pediment resembles a Grecian temple. One of the architectural highlights of the Cyrus Stafford House is the formal entryway with a re-cessed doorway flanked by Ionic columns.

The design was copied directly from a plate entitled "Design for a Front Door" in Minard Lefever's *The Modern Builder's Guide,* published in 1833.

The six-over-six sash windows are original. Rear porch and dormers were added sometime in the first two decades of the 1900s.

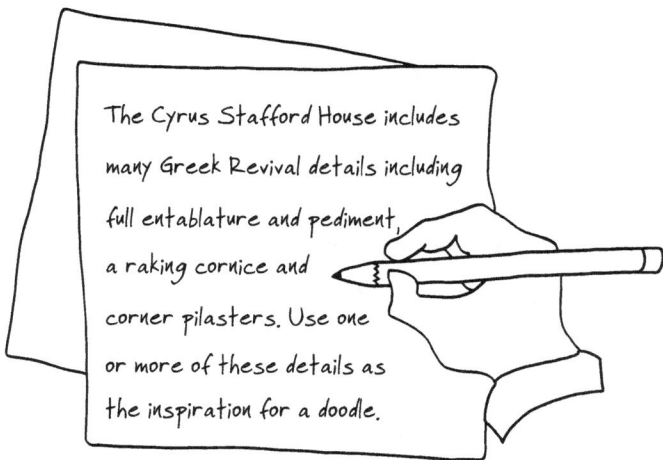

The Cyrus Stafford House includes
many Greek Revival details including
full entablature and pediment,
a raking cornice and
corner pilasters. Use one
or more of these details as
the inspiration for a doodle.

24. Henry Gould House

Situated on the corner of Main Street and Orchard Lane, the Henry N. Gould House is a red brick, two story, three bay, eve front, c. 1848 Greek Revival style house. Typical of Essex's flare for transitional houses, this Greek Revival was graced with an ornate wood portico introducing the introduction of trendy new Italianate and Gothic Revival details.

The exact date of construction and builder is uncertain, but the house was built on land owned by John Gould (owner of the c. 1833 stone Federal Style Stone house located directly across Main Street). Gould leased a lot to Charles M. Gifford in 1848. An 1849 deed transferring adjacent land from John to his son Henry Nichols Gould (b. 1818), references the southwest corner of Charles Gifford's Brick House. Henry married Sara Phebe in 1849 and was listed as having his own residence on the 1855 census. John Gould died in 1860 and willed all of his lands to Henry Gould. An 1861 deed from Henry selling this house states it was where he resided.

Was Gifford the builder, and was it a wedding gift from John Gould to Henry and Sara?

Many of the portico details remain, but the Gothic Revival railing once encircling its top has been removed for restoration. A similar railing adorns a street side porch on Beggs Park Lane! Can you find it?

Non-local white marble lintels and sills also highlight window openings of the Henry N. Gould House. Locally quarried blue-tinted Chazy Limestone provides its foundation and water table, and a monolithic slab of the same material defines the front steps. The limestone rectangle by the sidewalk is the top of a carriage stepping stone embedded two feet in the ground.

By Todd Goff

Doodle the portico with the railing restored (or doodle a different railing altogether.)

25. Noble Clemons House

The sort of ornate woodstove that may have been used to heat the Noble Clemons House once upon a time...

The Noble Clemons House sits near the corner of Elm Street and School Street. The Italianate building, an early but elegant palazzo-style residence, was built around 1850 for the then-owner of the Essex Inn.

The square, solidly built brick home has one of the first (and one of the only) flat roofs in Essex. Only the large decorative brackets supporting the wide overhanging eaves are visible from ground level because the roof is so minimally pitched. Crowning the Noble Clemons House, a lantern-style observatory offers 360 degree views of the Adirondacks, Green Mountains and Champlain Valley.

The ornate cast iron fence in front of the Noble Clemons House originates from the late 19th century.

The original six-over-six light sash remains in the windows. The cast iron fence in front is also a thankfully surviving feature that avoided being scrapped during wartime (WWII) metal drives.

Practical advancements in heating methods enabled the Noble Clemons House to employ a more open floor plan than earlier Essex homes. The first floor was built in such a way that it was open all the way to the roof top lantern via open stairways.

After being vacant for more than 30 years the house was purchased in 1988 and renovated with modern amenities while preserving its historic integrity.

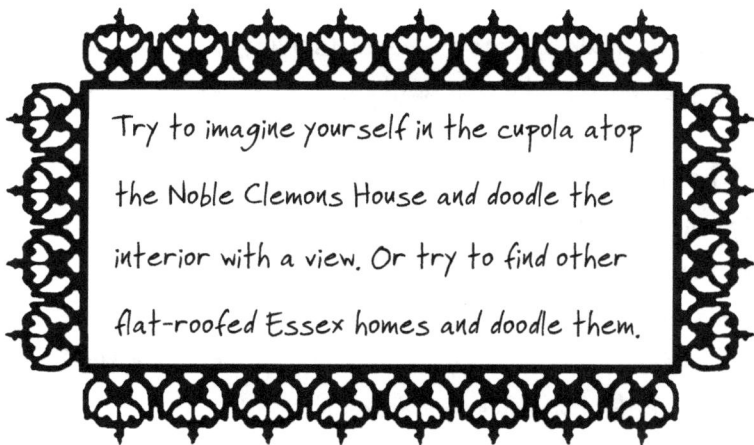

Try to imagine yourself in the cupola atop the Noble Clemons House and doodle the interior with a view. Or try to find other flat-roofed Essex homes and doodle them.

26. Essex Community Church

The Essex Community Church, located on the corner of Route 22 and Main Street, was constructed in 1853 for a total cost of $10,000 for the community's Presbyterian congregation.

The Italianate building was designed by architect T.S. Whitby and constructed of limestone quarried on Willsboro Point. The exterior combines roughly dressed, random-sized stones for the walls and similarly rusticated but uniformly sized, interlocking quoins to offset the building's corners. Large stone blocks frame the round-arched windows and doors.

The prominent three-story bell tower was constructed with round openings on three sides for the faces of a clock. But for half a century there was no clock in the bell tower. In 1911 Justice James S. Harlan and Maud Noble Harlan donated money

Italianate elements:
> arch-pedimented windows and doors;
> elongated 1st floor windows; and
> quoins (corner blocks);
> Any others?

to purchase a clock in honor of the recently deceased Adeline M. Noble. A century later the clock is still operational.

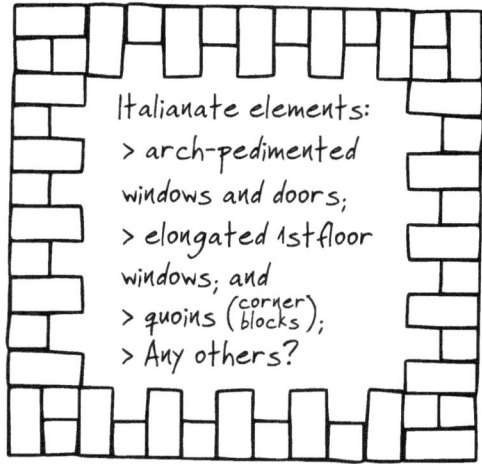

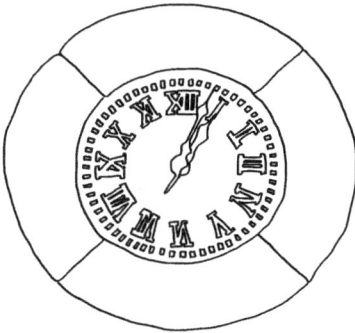

On June 20, 1922 the Baptist, Methodist, and Presbyterian churches united, creating one of the earliest federations of churches in New York State. They chose the Presbyterian's church for their new home, and it became known as the Essex Community Church.

Today, in addition to church services, the Essex Community Church hosts a popular summer concert series.

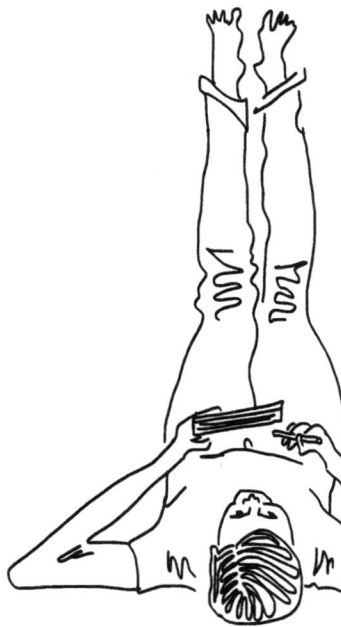

Doodle a view (or a detail) of the church from an unusual angle. For example, try sitting (or lying down) on the front steps and looking up at the tower.

Doodle Doors

Doodle your favorite entrance doorways in the village of Essex.

27. Greystone

Greystone, the newest and southernmost residence on Merchant Row (overlooking the Essex ferry dock), was constructed between 1853 and 1856 by Ransom Noble's son, Belden Noble.

This stately Greek Revival manse was designed and built by the same architect (T.S. Whitby) and construction team as the Essex Community Church. Locally quarried limestone was used for both buildings, but unlike the church's rusticated stone exterior, Greystone's stonework is smoothly finished. And instead of quoins, Greystone's

cornerstones suggest the presence of pillars.

Grecian temple details are evident on the gable ends, but unlike many Greek Revival buildings, Greystone is not oriented with the gable perpendicular to the street. Instead, the street-facing façade exhibits the same center entrance, symmetrical five-bay plan common to all of the historic homes along Merchant Row. As the last of the Merchant Row residence to be constructed, both choices may have been made to ensure aesthetic continuity of the Essex waterfront.

Over the years Greystone has undergone various renovations such as the addition of a south wing in the 20th century, but the Ionic porticoes on the front and north side of the house are original. Historic photographs reveal a wide parapet crowned with scroll and atheneum iron cresting that no longer adorns the front façade. The low parapet and iron scrolls were restored to the entrance portico in 1995.

Other iron worked designs were used on the exterior of the house, including grilles (of machine-stamped cast iron) that covered the attic windows. The ornate cast iron fence out front dates from the 1860s and matches the fence of the Harmon Noble House next door.

Doodle some of the embellishments on Greystone's exterior. Or make up your own that you think would suit the elegant home.

Doodle Questions

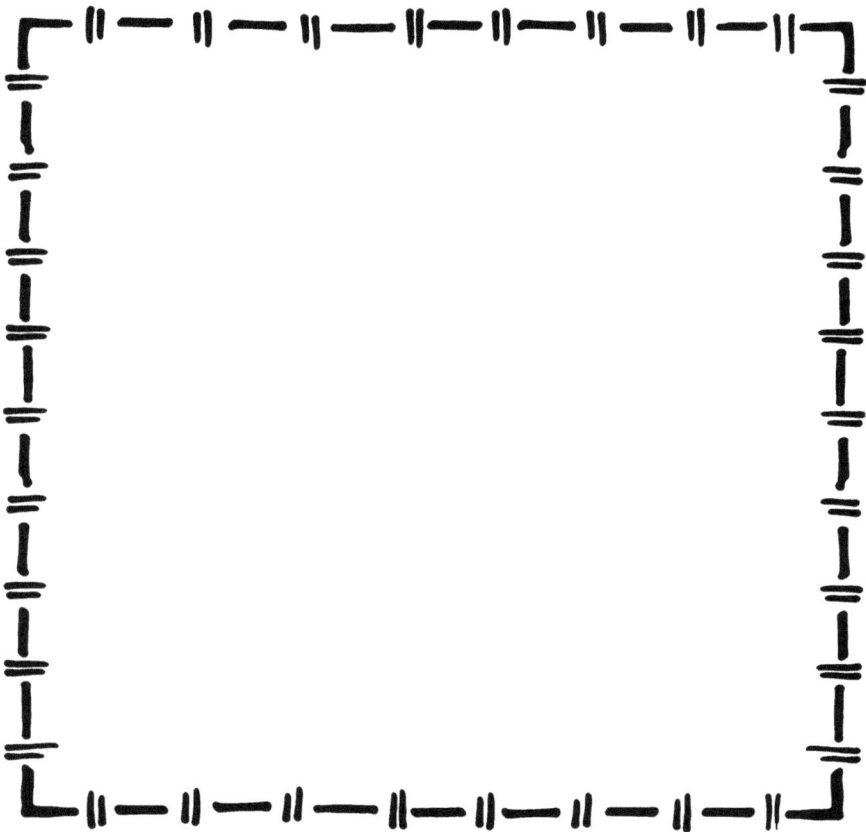

Doodle an Essex architectural detail that intrigues or confuses you. Scan/photograph your doodle, and email it (with a question or explanation) to Editor@Essexon-LakeChamplain.com. We'll do our best to find a (relatively accurate) answer for you! And we'll *probably* share your doodle on the Essex blog!

28. Harmon Noble Schoolhouse

This diminutive octagonal building presides over the Harmon Noble House's side lawn. The Harmon Noble Schoolhouse is an elegant, clapboard sided wooden structure. A steeply pitched Gothic roof supported by slender pillars covers the building and wraparound porch. The delicate pillars and the ornate wooden scrollwork (often referred to as gingerbread trim) spanning the eaves indicate a Gothic Revival influence, but the doorframes and window frames are of the Italianate style. 19th century Revival styles often mixed elements.

The Gothic inspired building is architecturally anomalous to Dower House, Rosslyn, the Harmon Noble House and Greystone. However, viewed in conjunction with Rosslyn Boathouse—another Essex waterfront anomaly—the two whimsical structures add balance and levity to Merchant Row's somewhat formal façades and grand proportions.

A small octagonal stone schoolhouse is located west of Essex in the Boquet hamlet.

The Harmon Noble Schoolhouse likely served as an 1850s office or a one-room schoolhouse, possibly used to educate the Noble family children. If so, it is one of two remaining octagonal one-room schoolhouses in Essex, although it is a very different one compared to the Boquet Schoolhouse pictured right (different eras, styles, origins, etc.).

Do you think
this tiny building
was an office?

Or a school?

Or something
else altogether?
Doodle your answer!

29. Union School

In 1867 the Union School was built on the corner of Elm Street and Station Street to replace the small Old Brick Schoolhouse. The school was constructed in the Greek Revival style (despite the declining popularity of this architectural trend), possibly to complement existing Essex architecture.

The partially restored building retains most of the original architectural details including clapboard siding and twelve-over-twelve window sash. The

original belfry features a Moorish arch roof (unusual for Essex) and weathervane. The fish was replaced with a replica in 2008. Two stove chimneys that once jutted through the roof have been removed.

By the time the Union School (aka Union Free School) was built, the population of Essex had already begun to decline. But the expenditure was deemed necessary in order to provide free, local education to Essex residents' children through high school. Previously students desiring secondary education had to attend private college preparatory schools.

In 1908 a new brick school was built and the Union School was closed. The building was rehabilitated in the 1970s, and has hosted several organizations throughout the years including the Adirondack Art Association, ReNew, Phillips Art Conservation Studio, and Historic Essex (formerly ECHO).

Can you find the "new" Essex High School that re-placed the Union School? If you can find it, doodle it!

30. St. Joseph's Catholic Church

St. Joseph's Catholic Church is situated about one mile north of the Essex village center. Construction was completed in 1873 by a mostly volunteer workforce at a total cost of $9,000.

The land was donated by James Ross with the stipulation that it never be used as a cemetery. For many years St. Joseph's has served both Essex and Willsboro parishioners, as the location made it convenient and accessible for residents of both towns.

Built almost entirely of locally quarried stone, this handsome yet modest church boasts a lofty cross-topped steeple remains visible from far away despite the fact that mature trees have dramatically altered the local landscape since the 19th century.

Road widening eliminated the rustic fence that once stood in front of the church, but the march of time was more generous with the Catholic church's windows.

"The eleven stained glass windows (including St. Joseph's picture in his carpenter's shop in the front) were installed in the early 1900s. Patrick Boyle, trustee at the time, chose windows that represented the joyful and glorious mysteries of the rosary." (*Essex, New York: An Early History*)

In addition fence and windows, history's plot evolved for the parish itself. Organized in 1872 by Father James Shields of Keeseville, St. Joseph's was a mission church of the Westport Church until 1910 when it became a mission of St. Phillip's Church in Willsboro. The Oblate Fathers took over 25 years later, and eventually St. Joseph's was once again paired with St. Philip of Jesus Willsboro, NY.

Doodle St. Joseph's Catholic Church from a different
perspective than the front entrance depicted
previously.

31. Wilder House

The Wilder House, located on the northern outskirts of Essex on the east side of Essex Road, was funded by the Noble family and built for Reverend C. N. Wilder of the Essex Presbyterian Church in the late 1870s. This brick residence was built in the Victorian Second Empire style, a French-influenced architectural trend that grew popular in America in the decades after the Civil War. Wilder House is the only example of Victorian Second Empire architecture in Essex.

Unique Victorian and/or Second Empire style influences are evident in the elaborate crown molding, the arched dormers and

mansard roof with fish-scale slate pattern, and the bay window on the south facade. Intricate scrollwork brackets and column moldings on the front porch are also Victorian embellishments.

Like many of early Essex properties, the Wilder House has experienced modifications and changes across time. For example, an elegant wooden fence once stood between the residence and the road, but it no longer remains. The southern porch was added when the home was converted into the Agawam Inn in the 1920s. As a business, it was most recently operated by Mary Gullo as The Essex House B&B. Today, Wilder House is once again a residence.

Can you transform Wilder House into a Federal style building? Look across the street at Crystal Spring Farm for inspiration.

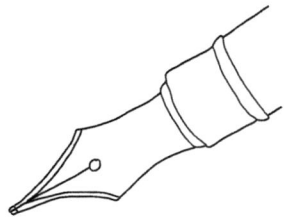

Carriage Stepping Stones

Have you noticed limestone blocks jutting out of the ground in front of some Essex homes? These carriage stepping stones or "upping stones" made it easier to dismount from carriages and other horse-drawn conveyances. As you explore the village document below any carriage stepping stones that you discover.

32. Rosslyn Boathouse

Built on a pier jutting into Lake Champlain this charming dock house was constructed around 1898. The Rosslyn boathouse is modeled on a late 19th century Eastlake design, considered part of the Queen Anne style of Victorian architecture.

Although the boathouse is part of the original W.D. Ross family property, it was not constructed by (or for) the Ross family. The turn-of-the-century building was most likely designed and built for the Keyser family

to accommodate their 62 ft. long, steam-powered yacht, *Kestrel*. Constructed entirely of mahogany, the yacht plied Lake Champlain's waters from the 1890s through the 1930s, becoming as much an icon of Essex then as the boathouse is today.

Popular boat races and regattas took place on the Essex waterfront drawing competitors and spectators to the Rosslyn boathouse and shoreline up until the mid-20th century. Boating regattas have dwindled, but Rosslyn boathouse remains a spectacular spot for viewing the Essex fireworks on the Fourth of July and watching the Essex-Charlotte ferry come and go year-round.

Doodle a boating regatta scene at Rosslyn Boathouse. Or perhaps "Champ" (Lake Champlain's friendly monster) inspires you more?

33. Essex High School

The former Essex High School, a square, brick and limestone building located on School Street a short walk or drive from the town center, was constructed in 1908. It remained in operation until the 1960s, and it served both elementary and high school students despite the misleading name. This was the last school that operated in Essex.

The Essex High School replaced the Union School that had been in use for less than 50 years. New heating, teaching methods,

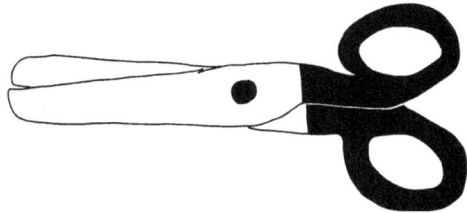

and educational advances convinced Essex residents that a new school was needed. The local school districts consolidated in 1952 and less than five decades after opening, the Essex High School closed.

Like the Old Brick Schoolhouse and the Union School, a cupola adorns Essex High School. The square, louvered structure rests centrally atop the roof next to a single chimney. The fenestration (a building's window design, proportions and arrangement) is another interesting detail in this Romanesque building.

Two first-floor windows on the front facade feature rounded tops and arched stonework, but all of the other windows are square or rectangular.

Try to doodle Essex High School's cupola
with a bell instead of louvers, or create a
composite doodle combining elements from
two or more Essex school buildings.

34. Van Ornam Building

In 1924 fire destroyed the Old Brick Block, a large mercantile building on Main Street. It was replaced by the current building in 1937. The Essex Post Office (previously located a few buildings north, next to the Old Brick Store) moved into the new building under the direction of C.E. Van Ornam who had been responsible for the town's Post Office since the 1920s.

Over the decades the Van Ornam family owned several Essex buildings (including Wright's Inn, then known as Adirondack House), but this central structure still accommodating the Essex Post Office today is most frequently associated with the Van Ornams.

Various enterprises occupied the Van Ornam building over the years, including a movie theater run by Gerry Van Ornam. It opened on Thanksgiving Day in 1940 with the film Third Finger, Left Hand. The space also served as the Atea Ring Gallery and more recently as the architectural office of Beverly Eichenlaub and Bryan Burke.

Today the Essex Post Office continues to operate in the south side of the first floor, and College for Every Student (CFES), a global leader at helping underserved students get to and through college, and ready to enter the 21st century workforce, occupies the second floor offices and rear annex.

UNITED STATES OF AMERICA

Doodle
a vintage postage
stamp of the Van Ornam building,
an architectural detail, or one of
the Van Ornam building's past or
present uses.

ESSEX-ON-CHAMPLAIN

POSTAGE ONE CENT

Sunburst Motif

"The firehouse's most prominent feature, the exuberant sunburst ornament in the pediment, probably dates from circa 1835. The Sunburst motif is seen occasionally on Greek revival pediments throughout the Champlain Valley of New York and Vermont, but the frequency of its early use in Essex is notable... One is tempted to speculate that the beautiful sunrises and sunsets over election plan somehow inspired its early use here." ~ Essex Community Heritage Organization, "Essex: An Architectural Guide".

The sunburst motif adorning buildings, windows, and gates has become emblematic of the Essex Village Historic District over the years.

In addition to architecture, the dramatic symbol influences local art and iconography. The influence is evident in local business logos including the Essex Fire Department, Historic Essex (ECHO), NEW Health, Essex Farm Institute and the Essex on Lake Champlain community blog.

"One of the remarkable assets of Essex is the adaptation of academic styles into a vernacular form known locally as Essex style, such as the distinctive Sunburst motif... actually derived from the fluted spandrel of the Federal period. Its use in pediment gables of the Greek Revival is an interesting regional development, celebrated today by residents of the town..." ~ David C. Hislop Jr., Essex on Lake Champlain.

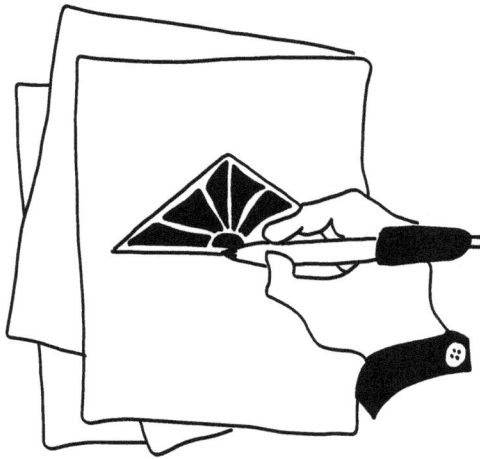

Wander around Essex and doodle
every sunburst that you can find.

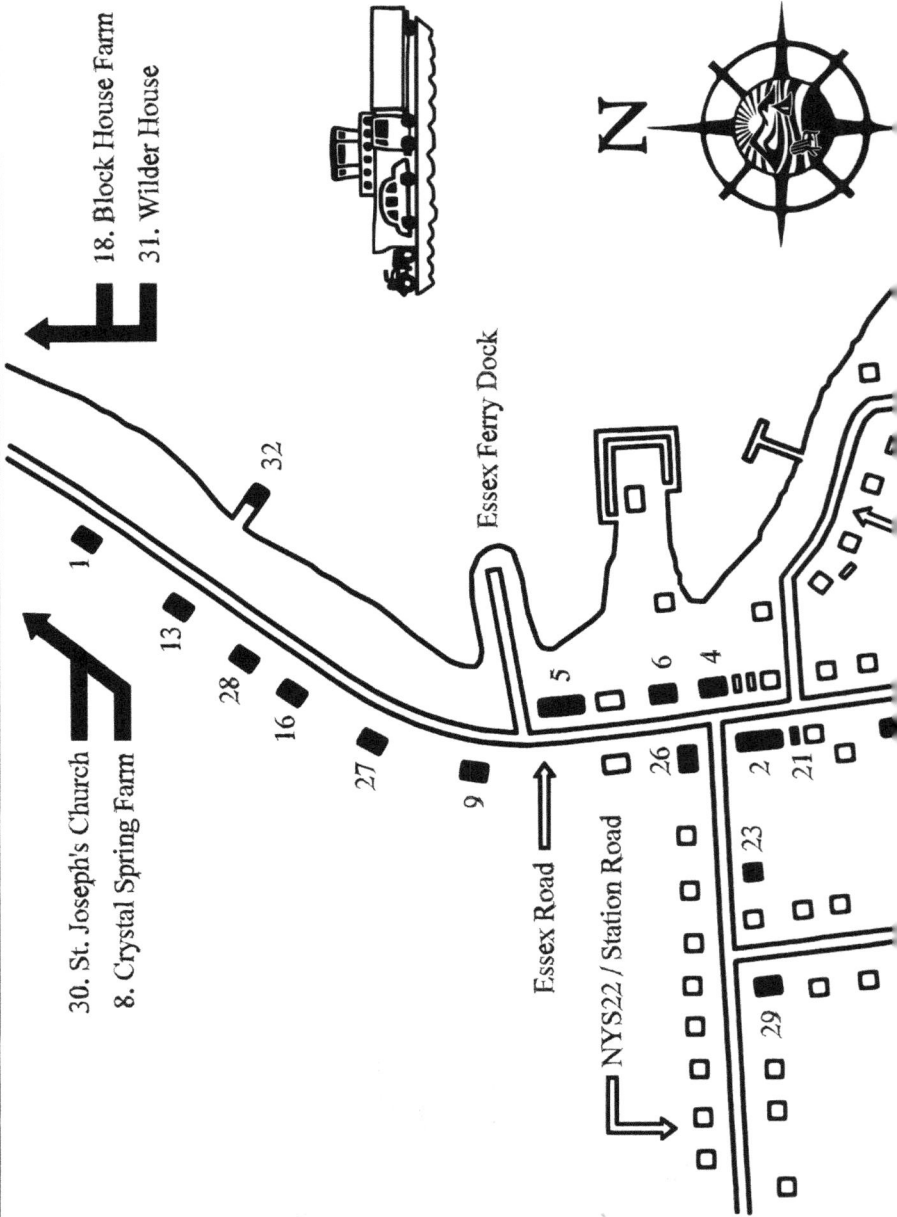

Essex - NY

30. St. Joseph's Church

8. Crystal Spring Farm

18. Block House Farm

31. Wilder House

N

Essex Ferry Dock

32

1

13

28

16

27

9

5

6

4

26

2

21

23

29

Essex Road

NYS22 / Station Road

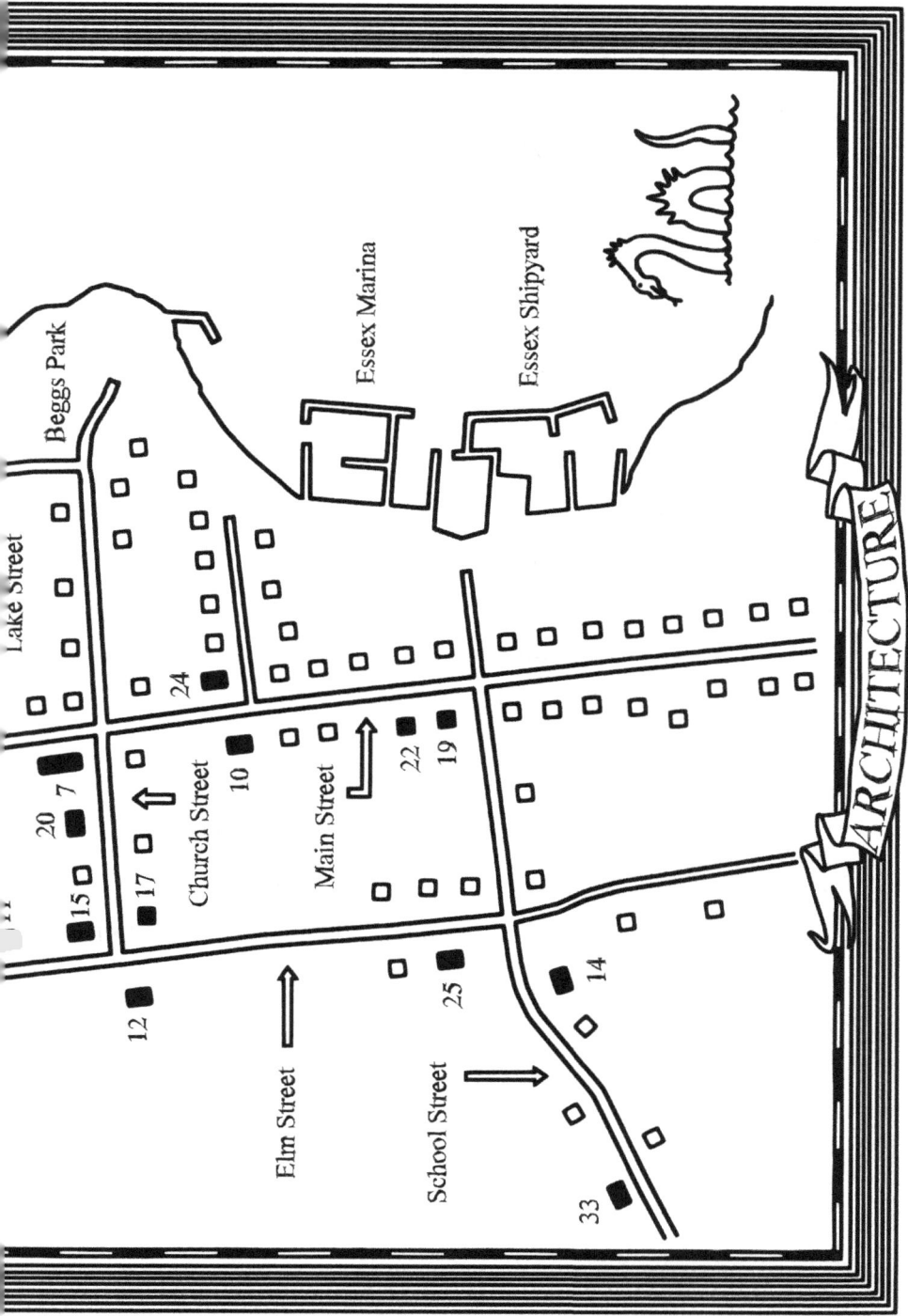

ARCHITECTURE

Beggs Park

Lake Street

Essex Marina

Essex Shipyard

20 7
15

17

Church Street

10

Main Street

22
19

12

Elm Street

25

14

School Street

33

24

Works Cited & Suggested Reading

Belden Noble Memorial Library. Essex, New York: An Early History. Burlington: Queen City Printers, 2003. Print.

---. Essex, New York: Lake Champlain's Historic Harbor. [Burlington]: n.p. 1969. Print.

Benjamin Asher. The American Builder's Companion. 6th ed. New York: Dover, 1969. Print.

---. The Architect, or Practical House Carpenter (1830). New York: Dover Publications, 1988. Print.

---. The Country Builder's Assistant: Containing A Collection of New Designs of Carpentry and Architecture; Which Will Be Particularly Useful to Country Workmen in General. Greenfield: Thomas Dickman, 1797. Print.

Brown, Sunni. The Doodle Revolution: Unlock the Power to Think Differently. New York: Portfolio / Penguin. 2014. Print

Everest, Allan Seymour. Our North Country Heritage; Architecture Worth Saving in Clinton and Essex Counties. Plattsburgh: Tundra, 1972. Print.

Harrison, Peter J., Fences: Authentic Details for Design and Restoration. New York: John Wiley & Sons, Inc., 1999. Print.

Hislop, David C., Jr. Essex on Lake Champlain. Charleston: Arcadia Publishing, 2009. Print.

Jones, Will. How to Read Houses: A crash course in domestic architecture. New York: Rizzoli International Publications, 2013. Print

Kleon, Austin Kleon, Steal Like an Artist. New York: Workman Publishing Company. 2012. Print.

Essex Community Heritage Organization. Historic Essex. Essex Community Heritage Organization. 2009. Web. <http://www.essexny.org/>.

Massey, James C., and Maxwell, Shirley. House Styles in America:The Old-House Journal Guide to the Architecture of American Homes. New York: Penguin Putnam, 1996. Print

McNulty, George F., and Margaret Scheinin. Essex; the Architectural Heritage. Burlington: Queen City Printers, 1971. Print.

Mudrick, Mary Beth, and Lawrence D. Smith. Federal Style Patterns 1780-1820. Hoboken: John Wiley & Sons, Inc., 2005. Print.

Rohde, Mike. The Sketchnote Handbook: The illustrated guide to visual note taking. United States of America: Peachpit Press, 2013. Print.

Smith, H. P. History of Essex County: With Illustrations and Biographical Sketches of Some of Its Prominent Men and Pioneers. Syracuse: D. Mason & Co, 1885. Print.

Smith, Keri. How to be an Explorer of the World: Portable life museum. New York: Perigee / Penguin, 2008. Print.

Ware, William R., The American Vignola: A Guide to the Making of Classical Architecture. New York: Dover, 1994. Print.

Westbrook, Virginia. *Relishing Our Resources: Along Lake Champlain in Essex County, New York*. Crown Point: Champlain Valley Heritage Network, 2001. Print.

Zimmer, Edward, John Mesick, and Janice Peden. *Essex: An Architectural Guide*. Burlington: Essex Community Heritage Organization, 1986. Print.

Acknowledgements

First and foremost I'd like to thank Katie Shepard. And then thank her again. And again! Without Katie's organization, discipline and gentle coaxing this architectural adventure would still be unwinding instead of binding. She's the MVP of the Essex on Lake Champlain community blog (www.essexonlakechamplain. com), and she's the ever-steady hand that ensures research, writing, editing and deadline-meeting continue even when I'm wandering and doodling. I'm fortunate, we're ALL fortunate, for Katie's smart and persistent "sheparding".

Behind the blog and the book and the storytelling is a parade of smart, passionate people whose research, stories, artifacts, advice and encouragement make it all possible.

Without question the Grand Marshall is Todd Goff. He's answered countless questions and shared personal and historic artifacts ever since I launched the blog in June 2011. His passion for Essex past, present and future is trumped only by his generosity. He authored most of the Ralph Hascall House and Wright's Inn sections and the entire Henry Gould House section. (The carriage stepping stone "treasure hunt" was his idea too.)

I'm deeply indebted and profoundly grateful for all of Todd's guidance. Thanks, Todd!

Lauren Murphy was another vital contributor. Lauren's generous revisions and insights dramatically improved this new edition. She combed through the beta edition, meticulously correcting, tweaking, and then answering our endless questions. Thanks, Lauren!

There are too many others to acknowledge everyone, but I'd especially like to thank Shirley LaForest, David Hislop, Diane Lansing, Morris Glenn, Betsy Tisdale, Mary Wade, George McNulty, David Glenn, Olive Alexander, and Ron Bruno. Absent your scholarship, memories, advice, and assistance there would be no blog and no book. Thank you.

At the risk of oversight (Sorry in advance!), I'd also like to recognize some of the extraordinary organizations and individuals that are catalyzing a veritable Essex Renaissance in recent years: the Adirondack Art Association, Alan Gardner

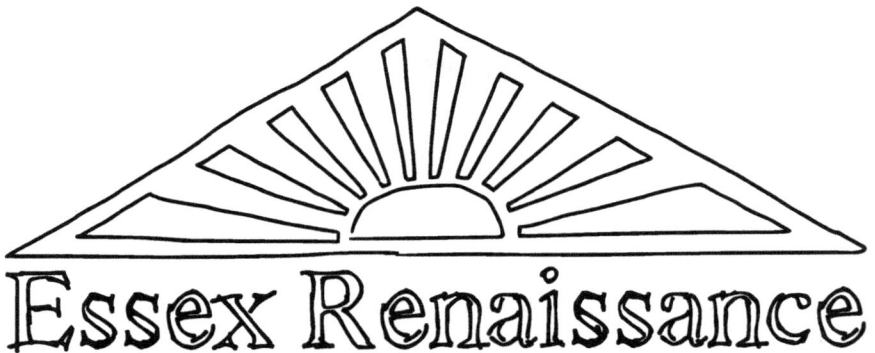

Essex Renaissance

Plumbing, William Bateman, The Bluebird Cottage on Lake Champlain, Sharon Boisen, Belden Noble Memorial Library, Cabins by the Lake, Champlain Area Trails, Champlain Valley Film Society, Chez Lin & Rays, College for Every Student, Cupola House, CvWireless, DAK Bars, Karen and Rick Dalton, John Davis and Denise Wilson-Davis, Emmet Carter Green Design, Essex Farm, Essex Community Church, Essex Community Concerts, Essex Community Fund, Essex Ice Cream Café, Essex Initiatives, Keith Castro and Lanai Monahan at the Essex Inn, Essex Marina, Essex Real Estate Co., Essex Shipyard, Tom Duca's Essex Yoga Club, Farmstead Catering, Flying Pancakes Catering, Fruition Orchards, Full and By Farm, Supervisor Ed Gardner, Grange Co-packer Cooperative, Greenhorns, Hall Design Group, Heritage Properties of the Adirondacks, Ron Jackson, Steven Kellogg, Kristin Kimball, Kristen Eden Fine Art and Photography, Lakeside School at Black Kettle Farm, Lake Champlain Yoga & Wellness, Lake Champlain Transportation, Tom Mangano, Maple Brook Farm, Carol and Nick Muller, Neighborhood Nest, NEW Health, Old Dock House, Pantoufs, Libby and George Pataki, Pedal Power, Phillips Art Conservation, Pink Pig, Pribble Excavating, Reber Rock Farm, The Red House in Essex, ReNew, Split Rock Farmhouse and Split Rock Lighthouse, St. John's Episcopal Church, St. Joseph's Catholic Church, the Whallonsburg Grange and Whallonsburg Civic Association. And so that I don't miss anyone, I toast everyone who's shared

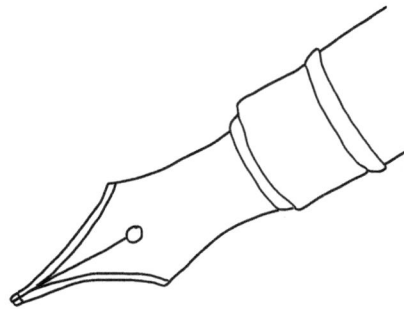

153

Essex miscellanea and encouragement over the past three years. You're the heart and soul of these Essex projects. Really!

On to geeky gratitude... It's time to shower some love on everyone/everything that made this quirky experiment technologically feasible and fun. The cheerful lettering (100% more legible than my chicken scratch) is generously contributed by João Faraco (Faraco Hand font) and !Exclamachine Type Foundry (Sketchy Times font). Obrigado! The doodles were created in a variety of ways, but any meaningful or useful images are credit to one or all of the following: inky, smudgy fountain pens and Sharpie (sharpie.com) Permanent Markers; SketchBook Pro for iPad (sketchbook.com) from Autodesk; Paper and Pencil by FiftyThree (fiftythree.com); Adobe Photoshop (photoshop.com); online-convert.com from QaamGo Media UG; and the ever miraculous iPhone and iPad. "O brave new world, That has such people [and doodle tools] in't!" (William Shakespeare, The Tempest)

My most profound gratitude is reserved for you, the reader and doodler. Your curiosity, creativity, and sense of humor complete the adventure. Thank you. Have fun!

Finally, a giant bear hug to my mother, Melissa Davis, who taught me that it's alright to continue doodling as an adult, and to my bride, Susan Bacot-Davis, who tolerates my idiosyncrasies and encourages my peculiar storytelling projects even though my "real" book still lacks a spine. I love you both more than words and doodles can possibly communicate.

Geo Davis, June 2015

Who the heck built this book?

Doodle yourself

_____
_____
_____
_____
_____
_____
_____
_____

Describe yourself

Katie Shepard is Editor of Essex on Lake Champlain (essexonlakecham-plain.com) and Box Office Manager of The Depot Theatre (depottheatre. org), among a host of other things. She is passionate about reading and writing and enjoys discovering more about her local Adirondack community by researching and blogging. Connect with Katie on Twitter (katshe77) or Facebook (katie.shepard.5)

G⁰ Davis is a storyteller who doodles, a flâneur who blogs, a global nomad turned "helicopter homeowner" (rosslynredux.com), a former teacher, a future poet errant, and a marginalia junk-ie (e-marginalia.com). One day George will sail around the world. Until then he lives in Essex, NY and Santa Fe, NM and online at virtualDavis.com.